*I have sometimes thought of the final cause of dogs having*

*such short lives and I am quite satisfied it is in compassion*

*to the human race; for if we suffer so much in loving a dog*

*after an acquaintance of ten or twelve years,*

*what would it be if they were to live double that time?*

— SIR WALTER SCOTT

# Angel Pawprints

## Reflections on Loving and Losing a Canine Companion

An Anthology *of* Pet Memorials
edited by Laurel E. Hunt

DARROWBY PRESS • PASADENA, CALIFORNIA

Library of Congress Cataloging-in-Publication Data

Angel Pawprints : reflections on loving and losing a canine
   companion : an anthology of pet memorials / edited by
   Laurel E. Hunt. — 1st ed.
      p.   cm.
      Includes bibliographic references.
      ISBN: 0-9660279-1-4

      1. Dogs—Literary collections. 2. Eulogies
   I. Hunt, Laurel Ellen.

   PN6071.D6A64  1998          808.8'036
                               QBI98-31

Typeset in Monotype Perpetua, designed by Eric Gill and released
   between 1925 and 1932
Period ornaments from the rare 1900 edition of the
   American Type Founders Cut Book

Cover and interior by Troy Scott Parker, Cimarron Design
◉ Printed by Thomson-Shore on Glatfelter acid-free paper

Darrowby Press
3510 Thorndale Road
Pasadena, California 91107

In loving memory of
MARMADUKE and MOLLY

*If love could keep them alive,*
*they would have lived forever*

# CONTENTS

# FOREWORD

# A Veterinarian's Perspective on Pet Loss

BY DR. ALICE VILLALOBOS, DVM

*Director, VCA Coast Animal Hospital and Cancer Center*
*Hermosa Beach and Woodland Hills, California*

THE LOSS OF A CHERISHED PET is a deeply painful experience. I recognize this daily as I treat pets with cancer and other terminal illnesses. Although we have made many advances in treating such illnesses, my goal in most cases is to preserve the pet's quality of life and the bond between the pet and owner for as long as possible. My job becomes twofold: to treat the illness, but also to prepare the owner emotionally for that sad day when the pet passes away. As I deal with the grief of pet loss every day, I have become keenly aware of the depth of its impact on the pet owner.

In earlier times, a pet's lifespan was limited by contagious diseases and accidents. More recently, improved health care and advances in veterinary medicine have increased pets' lifespans, but as they grow older pets also become vulnerable to cancer, heart disease, major organ failure, and other degenerative diseases.

Many of these senior pets have become cherished family members. Over the years with a pet, deep emotional bonds are formed. In my experience, most pet owners are unprepared for

the impact which their pet's death has, and the powerful emotions that they experience. They may focus on the difficult road
they have just travelled, and question whether something more
might have been done to save the pet. They may experience
anger, guilt, or depression in addition to the painful loss. Often,
they have nowhere to turn as they are afraid to openly express
their grief for fear of looking foolish.

As a veterinarian I am in a unique position to help my clients
deal with their grief. I have often found that the best thing I can
do is to acknowledge the person's grief in some tangible way,
such as sending a sympathy card with a personal note from each
staff member who was involved in the pet's treatment, or making
a donation in the pet's memory to a fund for homeless animals.
My clients have deeply appreciated these gestures, which let
them know that we, too, share in their loss. As with the death of
any family member, the grieving pet owner needs for others to
reach out, acknowledge, and validate their grief in order for the
healing process to begin.

I am thankful that a resource such as *Angel Pawprints* now
exists to help pet owners deal with their bereavement. This book
allows the healing process to begin by connecting the reader with
others who have also shared the sadness of losing a beloved pet.
The power of this book is that it touches the need to express
grief, a very important part of the healing process. The poems
and stories in these pages are so poignant that anyone who has
lost a pet, especially recently, will be deeply moved.

In addition to comforting grieving pet owners, this book will
be a useful tool for veterinarians and pet loss counselors. More-
over, it is a book to be shared when someone you care about
loses their pet and you want to express condolences. Sending

flowers seems inappropriate, mumbling "sorry about your pet" sounds inadequate, yet you want to do something to comfort your friend. To share *Angel Pawprints* is a thoughtful way to reach out to a grieving person. It is better than a card and more enduring than a phone call, and it reassures others that it's okay to feel sad when they lose a pet.

Ultimately, this book affirms the human/animal bond in a unique way. These timeless tributes and memorable photographs celebrate the special relationship that we share with our beloved pets, as companions on our life's journey. *Angel Pawprints* is a valuable addition to the literature of pet loss and healing.

# INTRODUCTION

THIS BOOK WAS CREATED from my personal experience of losing two beloved dogs, who died of cancer within seven weeks of each other. Marmaduke, a Great Dane mix, and Molly, a Flat Coat Retriever, had been adopted from a shelter seven years earlier.

Marmaduke and Molly were thought to be about two years old when they were adopted, so they were only nine when they became ill. At that age, I didn't consider them to be old or vulnerable to fatal illnesses. Thus, I was shocked to learn that Marmaduke was suffering from an aggressive cancer of the blood vessels. Although she put up a courageous battle against the disease, she had to be euthanized four months later.

Molly was a gentle spirit, and after Marmaduke's death I was greatly comforted by her quiet companionship. But on our walks I noticed that she seemed to tire easily, and tests revealed a large abdominal tumor. Only a few days after her diagnosis, Molly died from complications of surgery to remove the tumor. My grief at losing both of "my girls" so suddenly was profound.

Following their deaths I was comforted by the support of friends and family and by the sympathy cards that I received. One of the cards included a poem called "The Rainbow Bridge," which I found especially comforting. It was the beginning of my collection of pet memorials. Subsequently, I found "The Last Will and Testament of Silverdene Emblem O'Neill," written by the playwright Eugene O'Neill for his wife Carlotta, who was inconsolable following the death of their Dalmatian, Blemie. Over time, I collected a file of favorite writings, many of which I found in antiquarian dog books. I began to share them with friends who

had lost a pet, and my collection grew as friends shared their favorite pieces.

I realized that the death of a pet is a devastating experience in which one finds little guidance on coping. When we lose a human family member, we are allowed to grieve openly and are granted a period of mourning. When losing a pet, we often must grieve in silence and carry on as if nothing had happened.

Although I consulted books on pet loss, I did not find any that truly speak to the grief issues better than the simple verses penned long ago, which might ultimately be lost forever in out of print books. The power of these tributes was that they validated my heartache as a universal experience of dog lovers, allowing me to grieve. Thus, the idea of *Angel Pawprints* was born—an anthology of eloquent writings on the loss of a beloved dog that would comfort the person who has, in Kipling's words, "given his heart to a dog to tear." It is my hope that through this book, readers will find a measure of comfort in their loss.

In researching the material for this book, I discovered that the history of pet memorials and tributes is a long one, dating back thousands of years to the Egyptians who mummified their dogs.

Although some societies such as the Egyptians revered dogs, throughout much of history, many societies regarded dogs as a source of cheap labor and used them as hunters, shepherds, and

cart dogs. Around 1800, as society changed the role of dogs began to change also and they came to be regarded as pets, companions, and family members. Queen Victoria's fondness for dogs strengthened their  role as companions in the Victorian era. This coincided with the rise of the romantic period in poetry, which often expressed the Victorians' fascination with death and the afterlife. It became customary to hold funeral services for pets, and some tributes were penned especially to be read at such services. Pet cemeteries were established, one of the largest of which was in Hyde Park, London. The Hyde Park Dog Cemetery, pictured on page 156, held over 300 graves, many with headstones and epitaphs, when it was closed to further burials around 1900. Today, a pet's final resting place may be marked with headstones, plaques, or custom-carved inscriptions on river rocks. There is even a "Virtual Pet Cemetary" on the Internet where pet memorials are posted.

The majority of the writings in this anthology were written between the Victorian era and the 1930's. Where possible, I have included a date with each piece. When the piece was found in an anthology and the original publication date is unknown, the date is preceded by *circa*. I have also included a few contemporary writings that I found particularly moving.

The illustrations are from my personal collection of vintage photographs of dogs from the early 1900's. How cherished these dogs must have been to be immortalized in a formal studio por-

trait! One of my favorite photos accompanies the essay "Dear Dogs." It is a sepia-toned print I found at a flea market, which depicts an old dog sitting patiently in a chair in a Victorian bedroom while his mistress appears to be reading to him. Whatever the story behind this photo, it speaks volumes about the role of dogs in our lives as confidants and companions.

As I compiled the pieces, several recurring themes emerged. Many of the verses express the hope of an ultimate reunion with the pet in heaven. Perhaps the affirmation of this reunion accounts for the enduring appeal of "The Rainbow Bridge." Other verses speak to the feelings of loss of close companionship; unconditional acceptance ("this kindly friend...was one who deemed my humble home a palace"); emotional support ("Barney's love enabled me to do things I only imagined I was doing alone"); comfort in times of trouble ("a dog who would see me through the darkest of anyone's worst imagination of what the bleakest days would be like"); and simple joys ("I miss the circling welcome-dance") that every dog owner will recognize.

If you have lost a pet, you will find your emotions reflected in these pages. You will be moved to tears, but you will also smile to yourself as you remember "my dog was like that." You will discover a few pieces that you will re-read again and again for solace, because they speak to your particular story. Most importantly, you will begin the healing process.

Several of the pieces "written" by the dog contain the request to "not dwell upon my death, but celebrate my life." Accordingly, to serve as a memorial to my dogs by helping other animals, a portion of the proceeds of this book will be donated to animal shelters in memory of beloved pets everywhere. May this book help you to celebrate their life, and may their love always be with us.

— LAUREL E. HUNT
*Pasadena, California*
*December 1997*

**ND THEY** *shall be accounted poet-kings*
*Who simply tell*
*the most heart-easing things.*

— KEATS

# The Power of the Dog

RUDYARD KIPLING

1909

HERE IS SORROW *enough in the natural way*
*From men and women to fill our day;*
*But when we are certain of sorrow in store,*
*Why do we always arrange for more?*
  Brothers and sisters, I bid you beware
  Of giving your heart to a dog to tear.

*Buy a puppy and your money will buy*
*Love unflinching that cannot lie—*
*Perfect passion and worship fed*
*By a kick in the ribs or a pat on the head.*
  Nevertheless it is hardly fair
  To risk your heart for a dog to tear.

*When the fourteen years which Nature permits*
*Are closing in asthma, or tumour, or fits,*
*And the vet's unspoken prescription runs*
*To lethal chambers or loaded guns,*
  Then you will find—it's your own affair,
  But...you've given your heart to a dog to tear.

*When the body that lived at your single will,*
*When the whimper of welcome is stilled (how still),*
*When the spirit that answered your every mood*
*Is gone—wherever it goes—for good,*
You will discover how much you care,
And will give your heart to a dog to tear!

*We've sorrow enough in the natural way,*
*When it comes to burying Christian clay.*
*Our loves are not given, but only lent,*
*At compound interest of cent per cent.*
*Though it is not always the case, I believe,*
*That the longer we've kept 'em, the more do we grieve:*
*For when debts are payable, right or wrong,*
*A short-time loan is as bad as a long.*
So why in Heaven (before we are there!)
Should we give our hearts to a dog to tear?

# The Prayer of a Pup

WALTER A. DYER

*ca. 1935*

REAT GOD OF DOGS:

Seated on thy regal throne in the high heavens where ruddy Sirius flames; with all thy angel pack about thee, running to do thy bidding—St. Bernards and all the other canine saints, collies, setters, mastiffs and Great Danes, dogs who gained heaven through much loving and profound devotion, a noble brood, heroes of flame and flood.

Great God of Dogs look down and hear my humble prayer.

Outside thy portals this gray morn a little stranger waits, an Airedale terrier, nine months old, big footed, awkward limbed, rough coated with stubby tail held high, wagging rapidly, ears cocked and brown eyes full of innocent enquiry and pained surprise at his strange plight, pleading humbly for admittance.

That's Dusty Rhodes. He died last night in unde-
served pain. The tortures of distemper wore him
down. His little spirit passed beyond our ken. No
more our door is opened to his plaintive whine.
Great God of Dogs I pray thee let him in.

And if he cannot read his title clear to kennels in
the skies, I pray thee grant him mercy. If in his record
thou dost read much mischief and some disobedi-
ence, forget not his unsullied heart, his sweet smile
and gentle disposition, no trace of viciousness did
darken his young life, no evil mood nor any least
resentment. He teased our cat, but it was only play;
he would have loved him like a brother if he could.
And if on such and such a night or day he misbehaved
and heeded not the bidding of his mistress, on that
same day he licked the chastising hand and all was
soon forgiven.

There be no deeds of valor to record; but he was
young. He came of noble lineage. His little heart was
true. Be merciful I pray, and let him in.

His little collar hangs upon the nail, and even the
little whip, the sight of which chastises us today. He
has no home.

We cannot bear that he should wander there in outer darkness, unpatted and unloved. Is there no place in all wide heaven for him? Is there no loving hand to take his loving paw?

And if there be an angel child or two whose time may well be spared, some cherub who can understand a dog, who loves to play; I pray thee entrust him to his keeping. He will repay the care. Across the Elysian fields he'll romp and run; and if some angel stops and speaks his name, as neighbors did on earth, then there will sound the bark of pure delight that we shall hear no more, and heaven will hear a joyful noise that day.

Great God of Dogs, outside thy pearly gates this little stranger stands and begs the simplest boon. He only asks for someone he may love. Great God of Dogs wilt thou not take him in?

# To John, My Collie

WALTER PEIRCE

*ca. 1920*

S<small>O YOU HAVE LEFT ME.</small> *Here's the end,*
*My loyal comrade, fellow, friend,*
*You've had your day, as all dogs must,*
*Nor all your love and faith and trust*
*Could keep you with me—fellow, friend,*
*You've run your race and here's the end.*

*No not the end! For how shall I*
*Lay claim to immortality,*
*If naught your faith and love and trust*
*Availed to save your soul from dust?*
*Out of your brown eyes looked at me*
*A very soul, if souls there be,*
*And when at Peter's gate I knock*
*And Peter's keys hear in the lock,*
*And hear not any answering bark,*
*I'll face again into the dark,*
*From star to star, through God's wide space,*
*Until I find your dwelling place.*

And when I find you where you dwell,
Perchance in fields of asphodel,
Guarding white Elysian sheep,
One eye shut, pretending sleep—
But only one—and one ear cocked,
And chin on paws—though gate be locked
And bars be high, no gates there are
Can hold you back, nor any bar,
Nor angel with the flaming sword,
When once you hear your master's word.

Perhaps they will not want me there,
Perhaps not want you otherwhere,
And so once more our way we'll wend,
To outer darkness, friend and friend,
Nor lack for any light, we two,
So you have me and I have you.
And if perchance we lose our way,
Nor anywhere can find the day,
Together we will fall asleep,
Together sink into the deep
Great sea of nothingness, we two,
You with me and I with you.

# A Retriever's Epitaph

ROBERT C. LEHMANN

*ca.* 1916

 ENEATH THIS TURF, *that formerly he pressed*
*With agile feet, a dog is laid to rest;*
*Him, as he sleeps, no well-known sound shall stir,*
*The rabbit's patter, or the pheasant's whir;*
*The keeper's "Over"—far, but well defined,*
*That speeds the startled partridge down the wind;*
*The whistled warning as the winged ones rise,*
*Large and more large upon our straining eyes,*
*Till with a sweep, while every nerve is tense,*
*The chattering covey hurtles o'er the fence;*
*The double crack of every lifted gun,*
*The dinting thud of birds whose course is done.*
*These sounds, delightful to his listening ear,*
*He heeds no longer, for he cannot hear.*
*None stauncher, till the drive was done, defied*
*Temptation, rooted to his master's side;*
*None swifter, when his master gave the word,*
*Leapt on his course to track the running bird,*

*And bore it back—ah, many a time and oft—*
*His nose as faultless as his mouth was soft.*
*How consciously, how proudly unconcerned,*
*Straight to his master's side he then returned,*
*Wagged a glad tail, and deemed himself repaid*
*As in that master's hand the bird he laid,*
*If, while a word of praise was duly said,*
*The hand should stroke his smooth and honest head.*
*Through spring and summer, in the sportless days,*
*Cheerful he lived a life of simpler ways;*
*Close, since official dogs at times unbend,*
*The household cat for confidante and friend;*
*With children friendly, but untaught to fawn,*
*Romped through the walks and rollicked on the lawn,*
*Rejoiced if one the frequent ball should throw,*
*To fetch it, scampering gaily to and fro,*
*Content through every change of sportive mood*
*If one dear voice, one only, called him good.*

*Such was my dog, who now without my aid,*
*Hunts through the shadowland, himself a shade,*
*Or crouched intent before some ghostly gate,*
*Waits for my steps, as here he used to wait.*

# My Dog

## ST. JOHN LUCAS

### ca. 1915

THE CURATE thinks you have no soul;
    I know that he has none. But you,
    Dear friend! whose solemn self-control
In our four-square, familiar pew
Was pattern to my youth—whose bark
    Called me in Summer dawns to rove—
Have you gone down into the dark
    Where none is welcome, none may love?
I will not think those good brown eyes
    Have spent their light of truth so soon;
    Your wraith, I know, rebukes the moon,
And quarters every plain and hill,
    Seeking its master...As for me,
This prayer at least the gods fulfill:
    That when I pass the flood, and see
Old Charon by the Stygian coast
    Take toll of all the shades who land,
Your little, faithful, barking ghost
    May leap to lick my phantom hand.

# Roger and I

REV. JULIAN S. CUTLER

*ca. 1920*

ELL, ROGER, *my dear old doggie, they say that*
    *your race is run;*
    *And our jolly tramps together up and down the*
    *world are done;*
*You're only a dog, old fellow; a dog, and you've had*
    *your day;*
*But never a friend of all my friends has been truer*
    *than you alway.*
*We've had glorious times together in the fields and*
    *pastures fair;*
*In storm and sunny weather we have romped*
    *without a care,*
*And however men have treated me, though foul or fair*
    *their deal—*
*However many the friends that failed me, I've found you*
    *true as steel.*
*That's right, my dear old fellow, look up with your*
    *knowing eye,*

*And lick my hand with your loving tongue that never
  has told a lie;*
*And don't be afraid, old doggie, if your time has
  come to go,*
*For somewhere out in the great Unknown there's a
  place for you, I know.*
*Then don't you worry, old comrade; and don't you
  fear to die;*
*For out in that fairer country I will find you by and by;*
*And I'll stand by you, old fellow, and our love
  will surely win,*
*For never a heaven shall harbor me, where they won't
  let Roger in.*
*When I reach that city glorious, behind the waiting dark,*
*Just come and stand outside the gate, and wag your tail
  and bark—*
*I'll hear your voice, and I'll know it, and I'll come to the
  gate and say:*
*"Saint Peter, that's my dog out there, you must let him
  come this way."*
*And then if the saint refuses, I'll go to the One above,*
*And say: "Old Roger is at the gate, with his heart brim
  full of love;*
*And there isn't a shining angel, of all the heavenly band,*

Who ever lived a nobler life than he in the earthly land."
Then I know the gate will open, and you will come
    frisking in,
And we'll roam fair fields together, in that country free
    from sin.
So never you mind, old Roger, if your time has come to go;
You've been true to me, I'll be true to you—and the Lord
    is good, we know.
You're only a dog, old fellow; a dog, and you've had
    your day—
Well, I'm getting there myself, old boy, and I haven't
    long to stay;
But you've stood by me, old Comrade and I'm bound to
    stand by you;
So don't you worry, old Roger, for our love will pull us
    through.

# Jack

H . P . W.

*ca.* 1916

OG JACK *has gone on the silent trail,*
*Wherever that may be;*
*But well I know, when I whistle the call,*
*He will joyfully answer me.*
*That call will be when I, myself,*
*Have passed through the Gates of Gold;*
*He will come with a rush, and his soft brown eyes*
*Will glisten with love as of old.*
*Oh, Warder of Gates, in the far away land,*
*This little black dog should you see,*
*Throw wide your doors that this faithful friend*
*May enter, and wait for me.*

# Dinah in Heaven

RUDYARD KIPLING

*ca.* 1934

HE DID NOT KNOW *that she was dead,*
*But, when the pang was o'er,*
*Sat down to wait her Master's tread*
*Upon the Golden Floor*

*With ears full-cock and anxious eyes,*
*Impatiently resigned;*
*But ignorant that Paradise*
*Did not admit her kind.*

*Persons with Haloes, Harps and Wings*
*Assembled and reproved,*
*Or talked to her of Heavenly things,*
*But Dinah never moved.*

*There was one step along the Stair*
*That led to Heaven's Gate;*
*And, till she heard it, her affair*
*Was—she explained—to wait.*

And she explained with flattened ear,
Bared lip and milky tooth—
Storming against Ithuriel's Spear
That only proved her truth!

Sudden—far down the Bridge of Ghosts
That anxious spirits clomb—
She caught that step in all the hosts,
And knew that he had come.

She left them wondering what to do,
But not a doubt had she.
Swifter than her own squeals she flew
Across the Glassy Sea;

Flushing the Cherubs everywhere,
And skidding as she ran,
She refuged under Peter's Chair
And waited for her man.

There spoke a Spirit out of the press,
'Said:——'Have you any here
That saved a fool from drunkenness,
And a coward from his fear?

'That turned a soul from dark to day
When other help was vain?
That snatched it from wanhope and made
A cur a man again?'

'Enter and look,' said Peter then,
And set the Gate ajar.
'If I know aught of women and men
I trow she is not far.'

'Neither by virtue, speech nor art
Nor hope of grace to win;
But godless innocence of heart
That never heard of sin:

*'Neither by beauty nor belief*
*Nor white example shown.*
*Something a wanton——more a thief;*
*But——most of all——mine own.'*

*'Enter and look,' said Peter then,*
*'And send you well to speed;*
*But, for all that I know of women and men,*
*Your riddle is hard to read.'*

*Then flew Dinah from under the Chair,*
*Into his arms she flew——*
*And licked his face from chin to hair*
*And Peter passed them through!*

# "Just a Dog!"

## PAUL DE LOTT

### 1935

ITTLE PAL——
*No more you'll stand expectant at my door;*
*No more you'll wait my coming as before...*
*You're gone!*
*And folks said you were just a dog:*
*"There ain't no sense in fussin' 'bout a dog!"*

*How little could they know the thrill*
*Of your soft muzzle on my knee;*
*The thousand times my soul you'd fill*
*With your own song of ecstasy.*

*How little could they dream*
*That when men turned from me in scorn*
*With loyal eyes agleaming in the dark,*
*You kindled hope reborn!*

*Yes, just a dog—*
*No more you'll romp before me in the snow;*
*O tousled pootch, how little did they know*
*The resolution in my heart that you invoked,*
*The ache within me that your capers cloaked;*
*The human understanding that I oh so often swore*
*Was given to you in a measure more and more*
*Than any so called human that I knew!*

*You carefree tike;*
*You never asked for else but just to be*
*Where'er I wandered—up or down—*
            *'twas all the same to thee.*

*But now you're gone:*
*No more those ears will prick up in delight;*
*No more those eyes will shine their happy light;*
*No more you'll prance, and "speak," and strut—*
*Some heedless fool has seen to that, dear mutt.*
*And you have passed on to a place afar,*
*Where neither cats, nor cars, nor firecrackers are!*

*I wonder me, old friend, if 'way off there,*
*Where good dogs go to romp and skies are fair,*
*Will you await my whistle at the dawn,*
*As once you did in dear dead days agone?*
*And will you miss me, true heart brave and gay,*
*As I miss you, whom they call "just a dog," today?*

# Memorial

JAMES THURBER

1942

 HE CAME ALL THE WAY FROM ILLINOIS by
train in a big wooden crate many years
ago, a frightened black poodle, not yet a
year old. She felt terrible in body and
worse in mind. These contraptions that
men put on wheels, in contravention of that law of
nature which holds that the feet must come in contact with the ground in traveling, dismayed her. She
was never able to ride a thousand yards in an auto-
mobile without getting sick at her stomach, but she
was always apologetic about this frailty, never, as she
might well have been, reproachful.

She tried patiently at all times to understand Man's
way of life: the rolling of his wheels, the raising of his
voice, the ringing of his bells; his way of searching
out with lights the dark protecting corners of the
night; his habit of building his beds inside walls, high
above the nurturing earth. She refused, with all cour-

tesy, to accept his silly notion that it is better to bear puppies in a place made of machined wood and clean blue cloth than in the dark and warm dirt beneath the oak flooring of the barn.

The poodle was hand in glove with natural phenomena. She raised two litters of puppies, taking them in her stride, the way she took the lightning and the snow. One of these litters, which arrived ahead of schedule, was discovered under the barn floor by a little girl of two. The child gaily displayed on her right forearm the almost invisible and entirely painless marks of teeth which had gently induced her to put down the live black toys she had found and wanted to play with.

The poodle had no vices that I can think of, unless you could count her incurable appetite for the tender tips of the young asparagus in the garden and for the black raspberries when they ripened on the bushes in the orchard. Sometimes, as punishment for her depredations, she walked into bees' nests or got her long shaggy ears tangled in fence wire. She never snarled about the penalties of existence or whimpered about the trials and grotesqueries of life with Man.

She accepted gracefully the indignities of the clipping machine which, in her maiden days, periodically made a clown of her for the dog shows, in accordance with the stupid and unimaginative notion that this most sensitive and dignified of animals is at heart a buffoon. The poodle, which can look as husky as a Briard when left shaggy, is an outdoor dog and can hold its own in the field with the best of the retrievers, including the Labrador.

The poodle won a great many ribbons in her bench days, but she would have traded all her medals for a dish of asparagus. She knew it was show time when the red rubber bib was tied around her neck. That meant a ride in a car to bedlam.

Like the great Gammeyer of Tarkington's *Gentle Julia,* the poodle I knew seemed sometimes about to bridge the mysterious and conceivably narrow gap that separates instinct from reason. She could take part in your gaiety and your sorrow; she trembled to your uncertainties and lifted her head at your assurances. There were times when she seemed to come close to a pitying comprehension of the whole troubled scene and what lies behind it. If poodles, who walk so easily upon their hind legs, ever do learn the little tricks of speech and reason, I should not be surprised if they made a better job of it than Man, who would seem to be surely but not slowly slipping back to all fours.

The poodle kept her sight, her hearing, and her figure up to her quiet and dignified end. She knew that the Hand was upon her and she accepted it with a grave and unapprehensive resignation. This, her dark intelligent eyes seemed to be trying to tell me, is simply the closing of full circle, this is the flower that grows out of Beginning; this—not to make it too hard for you, friend—is as natural as eating the raspberries and raising the puppies and riding into the rain.

# To a Dog

ANONYMOUS

*ca.* 1916

N EVERY SIDE *I see your trace;*
*Your water-trough's scarce dry;*
*Your empty collar in its place*
*Provokes the heavy sigh.*

*And you were here two days ago.*
*There's little changed, I see.*
*The sun is just as bright, but oh!*
*The difference to me!*

*The very print of your small pad*
*Is on the whitened stone.*
*Where, by what ways, or sad or glad,*
*Do you fare on alone?*

*Oh, little face, so merry-wise,*
*Brisk feet and eager bark!*
*The house is lonesome for your eyes,*
*My spirit somewhat dark.*

Now, small, invincible friend, your love
Is done, your fighting o'er,
No more your wandering feet will rove
Beyond your own house-door.

The cats that feared, their hearts are high,
The dogs that loved will gaze
Long, long ere you come passing by
With all your jovial ways.

The accursed archer who has sent
His arrow all too true,
Would that his evil days were spent
Ere he took aim at you!

Your honest face, your winsome ways
Haunt me, dear little ghost,
And everywhere I see your trace,
Oh, well-beloved and lost!

# When I Died on My Birthday

KATE CLARK SPENCER

1995

Y HEART *broke for you.*
*I nudged your face while you called my*
*name over and over and*
*cried no until there was no sound.*
*You couldn't feel it.*

*Strange seeing your own*
*body lying on the grass. My*
*eyes were slits, my ears*
*black triangles. And my long legs*
*were tan and smooth as*

*polished oak. Not moving. You were*
*desperate, so I*
*gave you butterflies, the symbol*
*of the soul and of*
*rebirth. I prompted Kim to buy*

*a book of butterflies, gemlike,*

the microscopic
photographs, you said, dazzled you.
I got Max to grab
that tablecloth her mother made
embroidered in thread
with seven butterflies. Andy
made a cloth and wood
dog you used to show me. Yes, I
knew the dog was me.

Butterflies weaved into the silk
were rust-brown like me,
and iridescent. I was in
the canyon when a
butterfly followed

you along the creek where you found
my stone. And I watched
you press your cheek against the words
you had Kris sandblast:
BELL we will discuss butterflies.

# "Hamish"—A Scotch Terrier

C. HILTON BROWN

*ca.* 1920

ITTLE LAD, *little lad, and who's for an airing,*
*Who's for the river and who's for a run;*
*Four little pads to go fitfully fairing*
*Looking for trouble and calling it fun?*
*Down in the sedges the water-rats revel,*
*Up in the wood there are bunnies at play*
*With a weather-eye wide for a Little Black Devil:*
*But the Little Black Devil won't come today.*

*Today at the farm the ducks may slumber,*
*Today may the tabbies an anthem raise;*
*Rat and rabbit beyond all number*
*Today untroubled may go their ways:*
*Today is an end of the shepherd's labour,*
*No more will the sheep be hunted astray;*
*And the Irish terrier, foe and neighbor,*
*Says, "What's old Hamish about today?"*

Ay, what indeed? In the nether spaces
Will the soul of a Little Black Dog despair?
Will the Quiet Folk scare him with shadow-faces?
And how will he tackle the Strange Beasts there?
Tail held high, I'll warrant, and bristling,
Marching stoutly if sore afraid,
Padding it steadily, softly whistling;——
That's how the Little Black Devil was made.

Then well-a-day for a "cantie gallant,"
A heart of gold and a soul of glee,——
Sportsman, gentlemen, squire and gallant,——
Teacher, maybe, of you and me.

Spread the turf on him light and level,
Grave him a headstone clear and true—
"Here lies Hamish, the Little Black Devil,
And half the heart of his mistress too."

# Where to Bury a Dog

BEN HUR LAMPMAN

1925

 SUBSCRIBER of the Ontario *Argus* has written to the editor of that fine weekly, propounding a certain question, which, so far as we know, remains unanswered. The question is this: "Where shall I bury my dog?" It is asked in advance of death. The *Oregonian* trusts the *Argus* will not be offended if this newspaper undertakes an answer, for surely such a question merits a reply, since the man who asked it, on the evidence of his letter, loves the dog. It distresses him to think of his favorite as dishonored in death, mere carrion in the winter rains. Within that sloping, canine skull, he must reflect when the dog is dead, were thoughts that dignified the dog and honored the master. The hand of the master and of the friend stroked often in affection this rough, pathetic husk that was a dog.

We would say to the Ontario man that there are various places in which a dog may be buried. We are thinking now of a setter, whose coat was flame in the sunshine, and who, so far as we are aware, never entertained a mean or an unworthy thought. This setter is buried beneath a cherry tree, under four feet of garden loam, and at its proper season the cherry strews petals on the green lawn of his grave. Beneath a cherry tree, or an apple, or any flowering shrub of the garden, is an excellent place to bury a good dog. Beneath such trees, such shrubs, he slept in the drowsy summer, or gnawed at a flavorous bone, or lifted head to challenge some strange intruder. These are good places, in life or in death. Yet it is a small matter, and it touches sentiment more than anything else. For if the dog be well remembered, if sometimes he leaps through your dreams actual as in life, eyes kindling, questing, asking, laughing, begging, it matters not at all where that dog sleeps at long and at last. On a hill where the wind is unrebuked, and the trees are roaring, or beside a stream he knew in puppyhood, or somewhere in the flatness of a pasture land, where most exhilarating cattle graze. It is all one to the dog, and all one to you, and nothing is gained, and nothing lost—if memory lives. But there is one best place to bury a dog. One place that is best of all.

If you bury him in this spot, the secret of which you must already have, he will come to you when you call—come to you over the grim, dim frontiers of death, and down the well-remembered path, and to your side again. And though you call a dozen living dogs to heel they should not growl at him, nor resent his coming, for he is yours and he belongs there. People may scoff at you, who see no lightest blade of grass bent by his footfall, who hear no whimper pitched too fine for mere audition, people who may never really have had a dog. Smile at them then, for you shall know something that is hidden from them, and which is well worth the knowing. The one best place to bury a good dog is in the heart of his master.

# Only a Dog

FRED H. CLIFFORD
1935

NLY A DOG—*yet how he brings us cheer*
*And sympathizes with our many moods;*
*We love to have the little fellow near,*
*Regardless of the thought that oft intrudes:*
*"Only a dog."*

*Only a dog—yet with such constant powers*
*Of steadfast faith in us who love him so;*
*And when those trustful eyes look into ours*
*We know a loyal comrade's there, although*
*Only a dog.*

*Only a dog—yet can we turn away*
*And so forget the little canine friend?*
*No, never! for he hovers day by day*
*In close companionship until the end—*
*Only a dog.*

*Only a dog—and yet we grieve at heart*
  *When his cold form is laid away to rest;*
*And why not grieve, for it is hard to part*
  *From dear ones, though they be at best*
    *Only a dog.*

# Fetch

JIM SIMMERMAN
1989

HE MARROW *of it's this:*
*that night after night I dream*
*you alive, dream you clawing*
*up and through the snarl*
*of spade-lopped roots and loam,*
*through the cairn beneath the pine*
*in a bower of pines, a wildwood*
*of pines, beneath a wheeling moon—*
*shaking from your body*
*the tattered blanket, shaking*
*from your throat the collar*
*of blood—the ball*
*in your mouth where I left it,*
*your coat wet where I kissed it—*
*breaking through underbrush*
*onto the trail, tracking it back*
*to the tire-rutted road—*
*loping now, running now—*

*your nostrils flared*
*and full of the world—*
*ignoring the squirrel,*
*ignoring the jay, ignoring*
*the freeway's litter of bones—*
*night nearly dead as you*
*bolt for the lane,*
*up the drive, into the yard—*
*panting now, breathing now—*
*racing from door to window to door,*
*scratching at the screen,*
*whining at the glass, the ball*
*in your mouth—Lo,*
*wouldn't I shake from this*
*sweet gnawed dream to rise*
*and fetch you in*
*with the light that returns*
*me day after day,*
*takes you again and again.*

# To Boatswain

George Noel Gordon, Lord Byron
1808

EAR THIS SPOT
*Are deposited the Remains*
*of one*
*who possessed Beauty*
*Without Vanity,*
*Strength without Insolence,*
*Courage without Ferocity,*
*And all the Virtues of Man*
*Without his Vices.*

*This Praise, which would be unmeaning flattery*
*If inscribed over Human Ashes,*
*Is but a just tribute to the Memory of*
*'Boatswain', a Dog*
*Who was born at Newfoundland*
*May, 1803,*
*And died at Newstead Abbey*
*Nov. 18, 1808.*

# Going Gently: Love, Loss, and Death

SUSAN CHERNAK MCELROY
1996

INALLY THIS WEEK, after much prayer, I knew the time had come to let him go. So with the help of Pepper's friend and vet... I sat in our green rocker and, holding him in my arms, watched as the shot was given that eased him out of a life of pain and discomfort into one of peace and stillness. I hope he felt my lips against his head telling him how much I loved him.

I held him close and rocked him until the warmth left his body. Finally and reluctantly, I placed him in one of my robes, a well-worn blue one that still had my smell on it. I put Pepper's little red sweater on him; the ground is cold. And then I brushed his ears one last time. Between his paws I put two rawhide chews which he had once laid at my feet and gnawed on, and a yellow squeak toy which he used to bring to me, squeaking it loudly. And finally, I placed beneath him pictures of all of us, the people who had loved him. At his head, I placed a picture of him and me together. I don't need that picture anymore. It will always be engraved on my heart.

I buried Pepper beneath the Rose of Sharon tree in the yard. It's close to the house and I can see it from my kitchen window. Before I placed Pepper in his grave, I buried my nose in the soft top-knot between

his ears and drew in his smell. I always thought he smelled so sweet there, and I knew I would never smell that sweetness again. A river rock reads, "Pepper 1977-1992." On the porch near his grave I have hung wind chimes, masses of tiny, golden bells that tinkle softly when the wind blows. When I hear them, I think, "Listen Pepper, there's music for you."

# Lucy Never Had a Bone to Pick—
# She Loved Unconditionally

RUTH POLLACK COUGHLIN

1992

HE FIRST TIME ever I saw her face, she was six weeks old. Among her seven sisters and brothers, all of whom gained my attention, she was the only one who, when I picked her up, looked me square in the eye and then nestled her tiny head in the hollow of my neck.

I was sold, and she was for sale. It was 1978. It was December, and I had just turned 35. In New York in those days, I had grown tired of taking care of nothing more than a group of plants. Thriving as they were, those plants, they were not showing a lot of heart, and heart was what I needed.

Twenty-five dollars is what the animal shelter on Long Island told me it would take to liberate this creature, silky and black as India ink and a mixture of at least two breeds, with a minuscule diamond of white on her miraculously small breast. On the way home, in the car I had rented to drive across the bridge and bring us back to Gramercy Park, she curled her body next to mine and rested her face on my right thigh.

It is true that she sighed. It is true that I, a woman without children, attempted to understand that this puppy I had just named Lucy was not a child. It is also true that I could feel my own breast swell, my heart fluttering, my mind filled with the possibilities of unconditional love—mine for her, hers for me. Unconditional love: It was something I knew most people felt could only be doled out by a mother, even though many therapists acknowledge that family love, especially mother love, can be as polluted as the biggest and the baddest and the nearest toxic dump.

Lucy, in growing up, ate couches. She ate books and records and pillows and eyeglasses. She nibbled at fine Persian rugs. She ate shoes. She believed that the legs of very good chairs were her personal teething rings; she hid her rawhide bones in the pots of those well-tended-to plants, and then she would rediscover those bones quite dramatically, fresh dirt strewn across varnished hardwood floors. She scratched, and scratched again, at the surfaces of treasured antique chests.

Rolling against a tide of family and friends who castigated me for accepting such bad-dog behavior, I stood firm. She destroys *things,* I said. These things are nothing, that's what they are, they're things, they don't live and they don't breathe. She doesn't destroy people. She'll grow out of it, I said. People who destroy people don't ever grow out of it.

And, of course, she grew out of it.

Those who admonished me and never loved Lucy didn't know that for every new couch I bought, that for every pillow or pair of eyeglasses I replaced, I never looked back. They didn't know that Lucy was there during the times about which they knew not.

She was there when I cried, and licked the tears off my face; she was there when I rejoiced, and cavorted around, laughing with me.

She knew what was good and she knew what was bad. When louts were cruel to her, I comforted her; when they were cruel to me, her instinct was such that she curled tighter around me.

Even then, in those early years when the dog-expert books said I should scold her—and I did—she never stopped loving me nor I her. No matter what, she would finally smile at me, as only dogs can smile.

And always, it would be a smile that went beyond acceptance. It was much more: It was pure. It was without contamination. It was something called love with no baggage, something most therapists would not be able to acknowledge.

Away from the textbooks and the jargon, I was Lucy's god, and she was mine, a statement that has its ironic elements, insofar as I have not yet been able to decide whether there is a god or not.

She and I, transported both in spirit and in body by the man of our dreams, moved from New York to Michigan when she was five.

He grew to love her, as I knew he would, though at first it was slow going. Here was a man who had trained dogs all his life, and then here was Lucy— untrained except in one thing, loving me. He was the one who finally got it, truly got it, because he knew about a kind of love that held no barriers. Because he knew that this bond between Lucy and me was like our marriage. Incontrovertible.

When Lucy got sick on my birthday last month, exactly 13 years after the day I first saw her, I was optimistic.

For more than a dozen years, she had never been ill. Requisite shots, yes. Sickness, no. Romping and yapping and wagging her tail in her own inimitable Lucy way, she was perceived by the mailman, by the Federal Express and the UPS crew as a puppy. She was a dog who slept in the sunshine with her front paws crossed; she was a dog who was at my heels wherever I went.

She was someone who finally showed me the meaning of unconditional love. She was a dog who would never die, I thought, a Lucy who would continue to support me, who would be there, a dog who would see me through the darkest of anyone's worst imagination of what the bleakest days would be like.

We went three times, Lucy and I did, during those two weeks in December, to the veterinarian, surely one of the kindest and most compassionate people I have ever known. She was hospitalized, her heart failing, her kidneys not functioning, an IV unit hooked into her beautifully turned right leg, an inelegant patch marking where her once lustrous black fur had been shaved to accommodate the needle.

The vet allowed me to visit, but not for long, and from a distance. It might upset her to see you, he said, and then he added, if she actually does notice you, it might be disruptive for her to watch you leave. Not wanting to add to the pain she was already in, I peered through a window. She was listless, apparently unaware of my presence.

Maybe she couldn't see me, but she could still smell me, the person with whom she had been sleeping for 13 years, the person who could never tell her enough how much her love was valued. And how I knew, shrinks notwithstanding, that no one could ever get a bead on this, and if they did, they'd probably think it was bonkers and maybe they'd even have to go back to school to figure it out.

This was Lucy who was just barely hanging on, but evidently proud to do even that. My husband and I knew: She was very sick, there would be no recovery. She doesn't, my husband said to me, want to leave you.

Lucy and I went back to the vet.

He allowed me some time alone with her, the vet did, after he told me there would be no turnaround. This was a statement made shortly after the one in which he told me that it had to be my decision. Most people, he said, out of a need that is especially self-serving, prolong the lives of their dying dogs.

I knew what I had to do. Her suffering could not go on, not for another day, not for another hour.

For some time, I held her. I thanked her for being such a great pal. I kissed her repeatedly, on the top of her head and on her eyes. On her adorable nose and on her incomparable feet. On every part of the small body I had kissed at least a million times during the past 13 years. On her setter-like tail, even though she wasn't a setter, a tail that never stopped wagging.

On her heart that was failing, a heart that had beat so well, so true, a heart that could have, in a split second, taught a legion of therapists what unconditional love is really all about.

The other day, I somehow found the guts to open the envelope with the veterinarian's return address. Euthanasia, the bill said. Fifty dollars.

It seemed to me a small price to pay to allow Lucy, the one who showed me at every turn that she was all heart, to go in peace.

# An Old Dog

ANONYMOUS

*ca.* 1915

 OW THAT *no shrill hunting horn*
*Can arouse me at the morn,*
*Deaf I lie the long day through,*
*Dreaming firelight dreams of you;*
*Waiting, patient through it all,*
*Till the greater Huntsman call.*

*If we are, as people say,*
*But the creatures of a day,*
*Let me live, when we must part,*
*A little longer in your heart.*
*You were all the God I knew,*
*I was faithful unto you.*

# The Last Will and Testament of Silverdene Emblem O'Neill

Eugene O'Neill

1940

 Silverdene Emblem O'Neill (familiarly known to my family, friends and acquaintances as Blemie), because the burden of my years and infirmities is heavy upon me, and I realize the end of my life is near, do hereby bury my last will and testament in the mind of my Master. He will not know it is there until after I am dead. Then, remembering me in his loneliness, he will suddenly know of this testament, and I ask him then to inscribe it as a memorial to me.

I have little in the way of material things to leave. Dogs are wiser than men. They do not set great store upon things. They do not waste their days hoarding property. They do not ruin their sleep worrying about how to keep the objects they have, and to obtain the objects they have not. There is nothing of value I have to bequeath except my love and my faith. These I leave to all those who have loved me, to my

Master and Mistress, who I know will mourn me most, to Freeman who has been so good to me, to Cyn and Roy and Willie and Naomi. But if I should list all those who have loved me it would force my Master to write a book. Perhaps it is vain of me to boast when I am so near death, which returns all beasts and vanities to dust, but I have always been an extremely lovable dog.

I ask my Master and Mistress to remember me always, but not to grieve for me too long. In my life I have tried to be a comfort to them in time of sorrow, and a reason for added joy in their happiness. It is painful for me to think that even in death I should cause them pain. Let them remember that while no dog has ever had a happier life (and this I owe to their love and care for me), now that I have grown blind and deaf and lame, and even my sense of smell fails me so that a rabbit could be right under my nose and I might not know, my pride has sunk to a sick, bewildering humiliation. I feel life is taunting me with having over-lingered my welcome. It is time I said goodbye, before I become too sick a burden on myself and on those who love me. It will be sorrow to leave them, but not a sorrow to die. Dogs do not fear death as men do. We accept it as a part of life, not as something alien and terrible which destroys life. What may come after death, who knows? I would like to believe with those of my fellow Dalmatians who are devout Mohammedans, that there is a Paradise where one is always young and full-bladdered; where all the day one dillies and dallies with an amorous multitude of houris, beautifully spotted; where jack rabbits that run fast but not too fast (like the houris) are as the sands of the desert; where each blissful hour is mealtime; where in long evenings there are a million fireplaces with logs forever burning, and one curls oneself up and blinks into the flames and nods and dreams, remembering the old brave days on earth, and the love of one's Master and Mistress.

I am afraid this is too much for even such a dog as I am to expect. But peace, at least is certain. Peace and long rest for weary old heart and head and limbs, and eternal sleep in the earth I have loved so well. Perhaps, after all, this is best.

One last request I earnestly make. I have heard my Mistress say, "When Blemie dies we must never have another dog. I love him so much I could never have another one." Now I would ask her, for love of me, to have another. It would be a poor tribute to my memory never to have a dog again. What I would like to feel is that, having once had me in the family, now she cannot live without a dog! I have never had a narrow jealous spirit. I have always held that most dogs are good (and one cat, the black one I have permitted to share the living room rug during the evenings, whose affection I have tolerated in a kindly spirit, and in rare sentimental moods, even reciprocated a trifle). Some dogs, of course, are better than others. Dalmatians, naturally, as everyone knows, are best. So I suggest a Dalmatian as my successor. He can hardly be as well bred or as well mannered or as distinguished and handsome as I was in my prime. My Master and Mistress must not ask the impossible. But he will do his best, I am sure, and even his inevitable defects will help by comparison to keep my memory green. To him I bequeath my collar and leash and my overcoat and raincoat, made to order in 1929 at Hermes in Paris. He can never wear them with the distinction I did, walking around the Place Vendome, or later along Park Avenue, all eyes fixed on me in admiration; but again I am sure he will do his utmost not to appear a mere gauche provincial dog. Here on the ranch, he may prove himself quite worthy of comparison, in some respects. He will, I presume, come closer to jack rabbits than I have been able to in recent years. And, for all his faults, I hereby wish him the happiness I know will be his in my old home.

One last word of farewell, Dear Master and Mistress. Whenever you visit my grave, say to yourselves with regret but also with happiness in your hearts at the remembrance of my long happy life with you: "Here lies one who loved us and whom we loved." No matter how deep my sleep I shall hear you, and not all the power of death can keep my spirit from wagging a grateful tail.

# Maddy's Woods

JIM SIMMERMAN

1994

HAT CRUSTY, *good man John Fife*
*pretended to blow his nose....*
*In just one night her breathing*

*had grown labored, raspy*
*as a punctured squeeze-box;*
*her mouth cold, a pocket of ice.*

*I pretended, earlier, in the dark*
*back room, to follow the concise*
*lesson in black and white*

*textbook photos, in shadowy*
*x rays, back-lit, pinned to the wall*
*like the pelts of ghosts:*

*how the normal canine heart*
*is ovoid, a fist-sized egg*
*in the nest of the ribs;*

*and how this one's heart*
*had enlarged, swelled up*
*like an over-inflated balloon....*

*By now she could hardly walk.*
*By now she was wrapped*
*in a blanket on the floor,*

*and when she raised her head*
*once, to look around the room,*
*her eyes saw what?——*

*we might have been mist;*
*we might have been aspens*
*rooted in snow. It's time*

*to go walking in Maddy's woods,*
*where a hawk throws a shadow*
*you could chase through the trees,*

*where the tough, thorny branch*
*of a wild rose clings*
*to a little scrap of fur,*

*and all those smells*
*on the breath of the wind*
*make you crazy in the nose.*

*It's time to go*
*down on all fours and dig*
*deep into the frozen bed of the woods,*

*and let the heart rest*
*that ran so hard, that grew*
*too big for this world.*

# To Roxy

(Roxy of Lamar of Roscolyn)
by the one he loved best,
GRACE STRONG DIGNOWITY
*ca.* 1935

ITTLE PADDY *paws so quiet*
*That padded after me all day,*
*Eyelids closed in deepest sleep*
*Nor ever wake to play.*

*Shrouded in your red gold coat*
*That was your joy and pride*
*You'll lie safe from cold or sun*
*Where poppies grow beside.*

*You sleep my treasured little pal;*
*But what of me bereft*
*Of all your living meant to me,*
*With only memories left?*

The score or more of blues you won
   When gaily we would go
And share such fun and triumphs
   At all the big dog shows.

You tried so hard to please me
   And please the judges too;
Your manners in the ring dear
   Were perfect, just like you.

Loyal, loving, faithful, brave
   Until my saddest day
When you went alone your lonely road
   But here I had to stay.

Oh you will live on in my heart
   My little friend so true,
And memories of you fill my mind
   Until I go to you.

# Frances

RICHARD WIGHTMAN

*ca.* 1920

OU WERE A DOG, *Frances, a dog,*
*And I was just a man.*
*The Universal Plan,—*
*Well, 't would have lacked something*
*Had it lacked you.*
*Somehow you fitted in like a far star*
*Where the vast spaces are;*
*Or like a grass-blade*
*Which helps the meadow*
*To be a meadow;*
*Or like a song which kills a sigh*
*And sings itself on and on*
*Till all the world is full of it.*
*You were the real thing, Frances, a soul!*
*Encarcassed, yes, but still a soul*
*With feeling and regard and capable of woe.*
*Oh yes I know, you were a dog, but I was just a man.*
*I did not buy you, no, you simply came,*

*Lost, and squatted on my door-step*
*With that wide strap about your neck,——*
*A worn one with a huge buckle.*
*When bigger dogs pitched onto you*
*You stood your ground and gave them all you had*
*And took your wounds unwhimpering, but hid them.*
*My, but you were game!*
*You were fine-haired*
*And marked with Princeton colors,*
*Black and deep yellow.*
*No other fellow*
*Could make you follow him,*
*For you had chosen me to be your pal.*
*My whistle was your law.*
*You put your paw*
*Upon my palm*
*And in your calm,*
*Deep eyes was writ*
*The promise of long comradeship.*
*When I came home from work,*
*Late and ill-tempered,*
*Always I heard the patter of your feet upon the oaken stairs;*
*Your nose was at the door-crack;*
*And whether I'd been bad or good that day*

*You fawned, and loved me just the same.*
*It was your way to understand;*
*And if I struck you, my harsh hand*
*Was wet with your caresses.*
*You took my leavings, crumb and bone,*
*And stuck by me through thick and thin.*
*You were my kin.*
*And then one day you died,*
*At least that's what they said.*
*There was a box and*
*You were in it, still,*
*With a sprig of myrtle and your leash and blanket,*
*And put deep;*
*But though you sleep and ever sleep*
*I sense you at my heels!*

# Elegy for a Dead Labrador

LARS GUSTAFFSON

1980

ERE THERE MAY BE, *in the midst of summer,*
*a few days when suddenly it's fall.*
*Thrushes sing on a sharper note.*
*The rocks stand determined out in the water.*
*They know something. They've always known it.*
*We know it, too, and we don't like it.*
*On the way home, in the boat, on just such evenings,*
*you would stand stock-still in the bow, collected,*
*scouting the scents coming across the water.*
*You read the evening, the faint streak of smoke*
*from the garden, a pancake frying*
*half a mile away, a badger*
*standing somewhere in the same twilight*
*sniffing the same way. Our friendship*
*was of course a compromise; we lived*
*together in two different worlds: mine,*
*mostly letters, a text passing through life;*
*yours, mostly smells. You had knowledge*

*I would have given much to have possessed:*
*the ability to let a feeling—eagerness, hate, or love—*
*run like a wave through your body*
*from nose to tip of tail, the inability*
*ever to accept the moon as fact.*
*At the full moon you always complained loudly against it.*
*You were a better Gnostic than I am. And consequently*
*you lived continually in paradise.*
*You had a habit of catching butterflies on the leap*
*and munching them, which some people thought disgusting.*
*I always liked it. Why*
*couldn't I learn from you? And doors.*
*In front of closed doors you lay down and sleep,*
*sure that sooner or later the one would come*
*who'd open up the door. You were right.*
*I was wrong. I ask myself, now this*
*long mute friendship is forever finished,*
*if possibly there was anything I could do*
*which impressed you. Your firm conviction*
*that I called up the thunderstorms*
*doesn't count. That was a mistake. I think*
*my certain faith that the ball existed,*
*even when hidden behind the couch,*
*somehow gave you an inkling of my world.*

*In my world most things were hidden*
*behind something else. I called you "dog."*
*I really wonder whether you conceived of me*
*as a larger, noisier "dog,"*
*or as something else, forever unknown,*
*something that is what it is, existing in that attribute*
*it exists in, a whistle*
*in the nocturnal park one has got used to*
*returning to without actually knowing*
*what it is one is returning to. About you,*
*and who you were, I knew no more.*
*One might say, from this more objective*
*standpoint, we were two organisms. Two*
*of those places where the universe makes a knot*
*in itself, short-lived, complex structures*
*of proteins that have to complicate themselves*
*more and more in order to survive, until everything*
*breaks and turns simple once again, the knot*
*dissolved, the riddle gone. You were a question*
*asked of another question, nothing more,*
*and neither had the answer to the other.*

# In the Mansion Yard

## WILLIAM HERVEY WOODS

### *ca.* 1920

THERE'S NO NEED NOW *to look about my feet,*
*Or lift a cautious chair—*
*But uses of old years my senses cheat,*
And still I think him there.

Along the hearth-rug stretched in full content,
Fond of the fire as I—
Ah! there were some things with the old dog went
I had not thought could die.

The flawless faith mankind not often earn
Nor give, he gave to me;
And that deep fondness in his eyes did burn
Mine own were shamed to see.

And though to men great Isis, Isis is
But while she wears her veil,
This love looked on my stark infirmities
Life-long, and did not fail.

*And is it clean gone? Nay, an indian's heart*
*Have I, and even in heaven,*
*If heaven be mine, I pray some humble part*
*To earth-joys may be given——*

*Far down the ringing streets, some quiet yard,*
*Drowsy with afternoon*
*And bees, with young grass dandelion-starred,*
*And lilacs breathing June——*

*Across whose mossy walls the rolling psalms,*
*Like dream-songs, come aloud,*
*Shall float, and flying angels vex our calms*
*No more than flying cloud——*

*Some nook within my Father's House, where still*
*He lets me hide old toys,*
*Nor shames me even if foolish Memory will*
*Play with long laid-by joys.*

*There may my friend await, as once on earth,*
*My step, my hand's caress,*
*And nought of Heaven-town mingle with our mirth*
*But everlastingness.*

# Memories

JOHN GALSWORTHY

1912

...BUT WHAT A CROWD of memories come
back, bringing with them the perfume of
fallen days! What delights and glamour,
what long hours of effort, discouragements,
and secret fears did he not watch over—our black
familiar; and with the sight and scent and touch of him,
deepen or assuage! How many thousand walks did we
not go together, so that we still turn to see if he is following at his padding gait, attentive to the invisible
trails. Not the least hard thing to bear when they go
away from us, these quiet friends, is that they carry
away with them so many years of our own lives. Yet, if
they find warmth therein, who would grudge them
those years that they have so guarded? Nothing else of
us can they take to lie upon with outstretched paws
and chin pressed to the ground; and whatever they
take, be sure they have deserved.

*"Chris"*                                        MAUD EARL

Do they know, as we do, that their time must come? Yes, they know, at rare moments. No other way can I interpret those pauses of his latter life, when, propped on his forefeet, he would sit for long minutes quite motionless—his head drooped utterly withdrawn; then turn those eyes of his and look at me. That look said more plainly than all words could: "Yes, I know that I must go!" If we have spirits that persist—they have. If we know after our departure, who we were—they do. No one, I think, who really longs for truth, can ever glibly say which it will be for dog and man—persistence or extinction of our con-

*"When He Just Sits Loving"*  MAUD EARL

sciousness. There is but one thing certain—the child-ishness of fretting over that eternal question. Which-ever it be, it must be right, the only possible thing.

My companion tells me that, since he left us, he has once come back. It was Old Year's Night, and she was sad, when he came to her in visible shape of his black body, passing round the dining-table from the window-end, to his proper place beneath the table, at her feet. She saw him quite clearly; she heard the padding tap-tap of his paws and very toe-nails; she felt his warmth brushing hard against the front of her skirt. She thought then that he would settle down upon her feet, but something disturbed him, and he stood pausing, pressed against her, then moved out toward where I generally sit, but was not sitting that night. She saw him stand there, as if considering; then at some sound or laugh, she became self-conscious, and slowly, very slowly, he was no longer there. Had he some message, some counsel to give, something he would say, that last night of the last year of all those he had watched over us? Will he come back again?

No stone stands over where he lies. It is on our hearts that his life is engraved.

# Laddie's Long Sleep

JAMES CLARENCE HARVEY

*ca.* 1920

E WAGGED HIS TAIL *to the very last—*
    *And he smiles in his last, long sleep—*
*The troubles of life, for him, are past,*
    *In his grave, a few feet deep.*
*His soul—for I feel that he had a soul*
    *And he thought real thoughts, I know,—*
*Has found the ultimate end, life's goal,*
    *In the heaven where good dogs go.*

*He has lived with me and has suffered with me,*
    *Shed tears, in his dog-like way;*
*He has placed his paw at times on my knee,*
    *In a vain attempt to say:*
*"God never gave us that wondrous power,*
    *To tell all the things we feel,*
*But, I want to say, in my canine way,*
    *That my sympathy is real."*

*So I loved my dog to the very end,*
*And he in our daily walk,*
*Was never just dog, but a constant friend*
*And we had no need to talk.*
*And I hope, when the summons comes, for me*
*To embark on the unknown tide,*
*I shall find his eyes in the Paradise*
*They say is the Other Side.*

# So Long, Pal

ETHEL BLUMANN
*(on the death of Boy, my Irish setter)*
*ca. 1935*

WE'VE WANDERED TOGETHER
*In all sorts of weather,*
*The sun on our coats and the wind in our hair.*
*We've traveled the highways,*
*The streets and the byways,*
*In country or city, with never a care.*

*In summer's lush greenness*
*Or winter's gray leanness*
*Through fields, over hills, just you and I, Boy.*
*And stopping or going,*
*Or hasting or slowing,*
*My word was your law, and my will was your joy.*

*No hills' rocky steepness,*
*No roaring stream's deepness*
*Could stop your swift leap or your brave onward stride.*
*With eyes full of laughter*

*You'd watch me crawl after,*
*But always you'd wait till I stood by your side.*

*But we've come to the lonely*
*Dark crossroads where only*
*One may go on, and the other must wait.*
*Do you watch my feet blunder*
*With slow steps, and wonder*
*Why I linger so long, why I'm coming so late?*

*They'll be long years and hollow*
*For me, till I follow,*
*But I think you'll be waiting for me as of yore,*
*And then at our meeting,*
*You'll bark a glad greeting,*
*And we'll start out anew, together once more.*

# O Dog of Mine

ALPHONSE DE LAMARTINE

DATE UNKNOWN

...NO, WHEN THE LOVE *that lights up*
*in your eyes goes out,*
*It will come back to life somehow,*
*somewhere in heaven.*
*That man or beast, who loves with such*
*a tender sympathy*
*Can never die or be extinct for ever.*
*God shatters for a moment,*
*only to make whole.*
*For His embrace is wide enough to hold us all*
*And we will love each other as we loved in life.*
*What matters souls or instincts in His sight?*
*Wherever friendship consecrates a loving heart,*
*Wherever Nature lights the flame of love,*
*There God will not snuff out his divine spark*
*Not in the splendour of a night star's blaze*
*Nor in a humble spaniel's loving gaze.*

# Little Dog Angel

NORAH M. HOLLAND

*ca. 1870*

IGH UP *in the courts of heaven today*
  *The little dog angel waits.*
*With the other angels he will not play*
  *But he sits alone at the gates.*
*For I know that my master will come, says he,*
*And when he comes he will call for me.*

*And his master, far in the world below,*
  *As he sits in his easy chair,*
*Forgets himself and whistles low*
  *For the dog—that is not there.*
*And the little dog angel cocks his ears*
  *And dreams that his master's voice he hears.*

*And I know, some day, when his master waits*
  *Outside in the dark and cold*
*For the hand of death to open the gates*
  *That lead to those courts of gold,*
*The little dog angel's eager bark*
*Will comfort his soul while he's still in the dark.*

# "Dear Dogs"

LINCOLN NEWTON KINNICUTT

1915

EAR DOGS:————
I have brought together in my library a
few of the many proofs that show how true
is the affection which many of your masters have for you, and sometime when I
can read them for you privately, you will understand
more fully the place you hold in our lives. I use the
word MASTER only because our language is too
poor to express in one word the real relationship
which exists between us, we the master and you the
devoted slave and trusted servant, the most joyful of
playfellows, and the best of companions, the bravest
defender, and the truest friend. I wish I knew the
word in your language which expresses all that you
are to us. I also wish I knew how much you know,
and could learn the many things you would gladly
teach us.

You can see what we cannot see.

You can hear sounds we cannot hear.

You interpret signs we cannot read.

You scent the trails we cannot find.

You talk to us with your speaking eyes, and we cannot understand.

You are sometimes cruelly treated, and so are human beings, and sometimes we have to punish you for you are not always good. You have a certain amount of deviltry in your nature which we rather like, for it makes you more human and lovable. Your sins, however, are mostly against the laws we have made for you, not against your own, or those of nature, which are the laws of a higher power than ours—the one who made you.

What glorious times have we enjoyed tramping or riding through the fields and woods, over the hills and by the streams and through the swamps, or at the sea, on the sands and rocks, or over the salt marshes, with gun or camera or botany box, or with nothing at all! We have shared the best the world can give us, nature's gifts. And returning home, tired and happy, we in the evening, before a bright wood fire, you close by our side or at our feet so that you can touch us, have lived over what the day has given us. Or sometimes at night before a camp fire with the quiet of the wood sounds all about us, have dreamed of the ducks and the grouse and the partridges, or of rare flowers or a beautiful landscape which the past day has brought, or of what the next day will bring. And perhaps you have dreamed also, a little selfishly (you are only selfish in your dreams) of the rabbits and squirrels and the woodchucks which have been the greatest temptation for you to resist all day long. They must have existed long ago in your garden of Eden.

No matter what our conditions or surroundings in life may be you accept them gladly. King or peasant, palace or hovel, riches or poverty, plenty or starvation, burning sun or ice and snow, if you have once given us your affection, no matter who or what your master may be, you give him all you have to give to the very end—even life itself. It would almost seem that you were created only to serve us, for wherever man has been, even in the far past where history is almost a myth, you have been also, close by his side.

Old Egypt, Persia, Greece, and ancient Rome have told of your fidelity and of your devotion.

You know us in many ways as no human being knows us, for every hour of your life you wish to be near, and often you are our most intimate companion and the best friend we have in the world. We talk to you, more than half believing, or trying to believe, that you understand, and I am not sure but that to you alone we always tell the absolute truth, we whisper to you our secrets, we confide to you our hopes and ambitions, we tell you of our successes and our disappointments, and often in deep grief you alone see what we think is weakness to show to the outside world. Whatever happens to us we are sure of one friend, even if the whole world is against us. We trust to you our greatest treasures, our children, and we know with you they are safe.

When you go to the Happy Hunting Ground you are truly and deeply mourned, and the great legacy you leave us is the memory of your loyalty, your devotion, your trust, and memory of the many happy hours and happy days you have given us in your too short life. And when we are obliged to say "the King is dead," we do not complete the old saying "long live the King" for many, many months—and sometimes never.

May we meet again,
Your masters, and
Your FRIENDS

# To Sigourd

KATHERINE LEE BATES

*ca. 1920*

OT ONE BLITHE LEAP *of welcome? Can you lie*
*Under this woodland mold,*
*More still*
*Than broken daffodil,*
*When I,*
*Home from too long a roving,*
*Come up the silent hill?*
*Dear, wistful eyes,*
*White ruff and windy gold*
*Of collie coat so oft caressed,*
*Not one quick thrill*
*In snowy breast,*
*One spring of jubilant surprise,*
*One ecstasy of loving?*

*Are all our frolics ended? Never more*
*Those royal romps of old,*
*When one,*

*Playfellow of the sun,*
*Would pour*
*Adventures and romances*
*Into a morning run;*

*Off and away,*
*A flying glint of gold,*
*Startling to wing a husky choir*
*Of crows whose dun*
*Shadows would tire*
*Even that wild speed? Unscared to-day*
*They hold their weird seances.*

*Ever you dreamed, legs twitching, you*
  *would catch*
*A crow, O leaper bold,*
*Next time,——*
*Or chase to branch sublime*
*That batch*
*Of squirrels daring capture*
*In saucy pantomime;*
*Till one spring dawn,*
*Resting amid the gold*
*Of crocuses, Death stole on you*
*From that far clime*
*Where dreams come true,*
*And left upon the starry lawn*
*Your form without your rapture.*

*And was Death's whistle then so wondrous*
  *sweet*
*Across the glimmering wold*
*That you*
*Would trustfully pursue*
*Strange feet?*
*When I was gone, each morrow*
*You sought our old haunts through,*

*Slower to play,*
*Drooping in faded gold.*
*Now it is mine to grieve and miss*
*My comrade true,*
*Who used to kiss*
*With eager tongue such tears away,*
*Coaxing a smile from sorrow.*

*I know not what life is, nor what is death,*
*Nor how vast Heaven may hold*
*All this*
*Earth-beauty and earth-bliss.*
*Christ saith*
*That not a sparrow falleth*
*—O songs of sparrow faith!—*
*But God is there.*
*May not a leap of gold*
*Yet greet me on some gladder hill,*
*A shining wraith,*
*Rejoicing still,*
*As in those hours we found so fair,*
*To follow where love calleth?*

# Death of a Dog

H.I. PHILLIPS

1955

 HE HAD SLUMPED from a sofa and dragged her tired body toward a thin slant of autumn's golden sunlight on the dark rug. It seemed as if she had tried to reach and capture it, and we knew that if she had done so, it would be only to give it back in some way, just as she had returned all warmth and light and love.

Now she lay there on her side, inert and with wide eyes staring ahead. It was as if she had entered the dog Valhalla to hear the voice of children and the cry of "Fetch it." There was infinite peace in her form, and it lessened the heartbreak to know she had gone as if to sleep after sixteen full years as part of your life and household.

Peppy never again would be seen at the window at the footstep of a returning loved one, ready to bestow the frenzied welcome only a pooch can give.

It was hard to realize there would be no more breath-less scamperings around the house in the ecstasy of a homecoming, as deep after a ten-minute trip to the stores as after a month in some other city.

Peppy, as a toy bull, had come to us as a puppy. She had the rugged vitality and courage of the male, rather than the female, animal. And through the years which she helped to make lovely she had known a vigorous health which had suddenly gone to pieces like the "one hoss shay."

For a week she lay weak and wondering, only her ears alert to footsteps and shouts of kids in the fields. She had given all she could to her master, but it was to her mistress that she had always awarded the match-less adoration and worship. The missus couldn't step from one room to another without her following just to be near. A minute was an ordeal of solitude for this brindle and white bundle of devotion. It was good to know the last voice she heard and the last face she saw had been that of her mistress, now in tears beside her.

Peppy had given her all ceaselessly from the day she crawled out of a wicker basket, and the special angels which reward the ultimate love had seen her going was without pain. The missus and I like to

think they carried her swiftly to the Valhalla of wonderful animals and that scarcely had her heart
stopped beating before she was a frisky puppy again.
Much can be given to her up there...and Peppy will
give it all back with interest.

# The Passing of a Dog

ANONYMOUS

*ca.* 1916

HIS KINDLY FRIEND *of mine who's passed*
*Beyond the realm of day,*
*Beyond the realm of darkling night,*
*To unknown bourne away*

*Was one who deemed my humble home*
*A palace grand and fair;*
*Whose fullest joy it was to find*
*His comrade ever there.*

*Ah! He has gone from out my life*
*Like some dear dream I knew.*
*A man may own a hundred dogs,*
*But one he loves, and true.*

# In Memoriam

HENRY WILLETT

*ca.* 1916

 MISS THE *little wagging tail;*
*I miss the plaintive, pleading wail;*
*I miss the wistful, loving glance;*
*I miss the circling welcome-dance.*

*I miss the eyes that, watching, sued;*
*I miss her tongue of gratitude*
*That licked my hand, in loving mood,*
*When we divided cup or food.*

*I miss the pertinacious scratch*
*(Continued till I raised the latch*
*Each morning), waiting at my door;*
*Alas, I ne'er shall hear it more.*

*"What folly!" hints the cynic mind,*
*"Plenty of dogs are left behind*
*To snap and snarl, to bark and bite,*
*And wake us in the gloomy night.*

*"You should have sought a human friend,*
*Whose life eternal ne'er could end—*
*Whose gifts of intellect and grace*
*Bereavement never could efface."*

*Plenty of snarling things are left,*
*But I am of a friend bereft;*
*I seek not intellect, but heart—*
*'Tis not my head that feels the smart.*

*While loving sympathy is cherished,*
*While gratitude is not quite perished;*
*While patient, hopeful, cheerful meeting*
*At our return is pleasant greeting;*

*So long my heart will feel a void—*
*Grieving, my mind will be employed—*
*When I, returning to my door,*
*Shall miss what I shall find no more.*

*When we, at last, shall pass away,*
*And see no more the light of day,*
*Will many hearts as vacant mourn—*
*As truly wish for our return?*

Yet love that's true will ever know
The pain of parting. Better so!
"Better to love and lose" than cold,
And colder still, let hearts grow old.

So let the cynic snarl or smile,
And his great intellect beguile;
My little dog, so true to me,
Will dear to heart and memory be.

# The Barney Years (excerpt)

JOHN D. RUCKER

1992

 URING THE EARLY BARNEY YEARS, I had no home. I was driven by the search for "the moment," in the sense of fishing for excitement, for beauty, for the opportunity to test one's self, for the revealed glimpses of the essential truth of our existence.... In 1979, tragedy struck my family back in North Carolina.

My mother's death came in October, and my father's health began to fail almost immediately. I began to spend much of the year in North Carolina. At first I felt I was giving up the things that made life worth living—the good fishing and hunting—but by the mid-1980's North Carolina was home again....

As for Barney, North Carolina must have been a place of dazzling sensuousness. In the evenings of early spring, I would watch him where he was tied in the shade in the front yard. Here he kept my van under surveillance, to ensure that he was not left behind on any outing.

He would stare into the splendid hardwoods in my father's front yard, listening to the jar flies and katydids as they droned in the leafy canopy high over-head. He watched incredulously as lightning bugs blinked off and on in the twilight. The smells of the subtropical hardwood and pine forest were so foreign to Barney, so lush, and the nights so humid and still, that he must have known he had been taken to a vastly different place by his lord and master.

I think he knew as well that it was my father who spoke softly in the yard, and that all was not right with him, and that our purpose there was connected with him. Barney knew that there were three worlds after 1979. One was where he sat at the feet of my father and me, as we sat on the porch engaging in much conversation and laughter.

Each May we began an odyssey of truly epic pro-portions, back to the world at the other end. Barney and I would drive from North Carolina to Montana, fly fish for a week, then continue to Seattle, where we stored the van. We then flew to Alaska for the com-mercial fishing season, which usually lasted four months....

On his leash, Barney would walk down the steps of the Twin Otter in early May or June, a week before commercial fishing, and smell the Bering Sea air, sled dogs, and salmon on the racks. His expression would say, "Oh, we're in one of the other worlds again—the fish world."

In October we would drive from Seattle to Montana, the place of Hungarian partridge, pheasants, and brook trout—the "middle world" or the "bird place." Each December found us back in North Carolina again—the "homeplace."

This went on till the winter of 1987. That was when I learned that Barney had cancer. An anal gland at the base of his tail had become hard and impacted, and was malignant. Barney was accepted at the North Carolina State University Vet School, one of the best in the country, for experimental radiation treatment. Twice a week for eight weeks, I drove one hundred miles to Raleigh, where Barney was put to sleep and irradiated.

The fur fell out on his rump. The flesh became red and angry. Usually, somewhere between Burlington and Greensboro, the anesthesia wore off and Barney would stir in the front seat. I would wake him with a gentle hand on the top of his head, since he was nearly deaf by then, at the age of thirteen and a half. The stub of a tail would wag three times, no more, when he realized he was with me again....

Barney's treatment was concluded in late October. There was only time to fly to North Dakota for a ten-day bird hunt. The treatment may have helped give Barney strength for that last trip. I will never know for certain if it made a difference, but I do not feel it was worth the torture that he so uncomplainingly endured.

He hunted passionately. His eyes glowed that last fall, questing for the golden scent, the moment of the flush, the pop of the gun, the bearing of the prize back to my hand. I dreaded the last day of hunting, for I knew what Barney could not know—that there would never be another autumn for him....

That last day before the flight out of Bismarck, I hunted sharp-tailed grouse west of Dickinson. At day's end we hunted in a deep coulee, where very cold air had settled in. Barney's breath came out in white puffs. At sundown he ran ahead and flushed a flock of grouse, but they were slightly out of range. He sat down and waited for me. The look on his face said, "I got a little ahead of the gun." He was slightly embarrassed, and utterly human.

At the top of the coulee, a flock of sharptails on their way to roost flew directly overhead. I killed one bird and Barney bounded to it, his red rump and naked tail wagging furiously. He brought it to me with his head held high, eyes blazing. I took the bird from him and sat in the dried, brown grass and cried, long and long. He watched me gravely, the prairie wind ruffling his fur.

As the year turned over and 1988 began, Barney had difficulty passing stools. A tumor inside his abdomen was gradually blocking off his small intestine. There was nothing to be done. One Sunday I had no inclination to leave the house. I lay in bed and read, and Barney, who usually preferred to have his own space, joined me on the bed. We visited amiably, my hand on his head as I read.

That night around midnight, he woke me up with cries of pain. When I picked him up, he cried like a child, looking frantically into my eyes. I took him to an emergency vet clinic, where he was sedated. The next morning, the vet told me that Barney's time was up. Joy and I sat on the floor in the back room for hours, stroking him where he lay in the kennel. He would doze off to sleep, then lift his head and look at Joy and me and put his head down again, reassured.

Finally, when it was after closing hours, there was nothing left to do. I would hold Barney in my arms as the shot was given. Barney and I would see this last thing through to the end together, for Barney never had any patience with faintheartedness. As Barney dozed in my arms, I gazed at him one last time, and images that spanned a continent flashed by. When I saw Barney was in deep sleep, I nodded my head. He would never wake from this last dream.

But Barney would not "go gentle into that good night." When the serum hit his bloodstream, it must have registered very hot, for he jerked his head erect, pulling it from my arms, and bit me on the hand, eyes crying out, "Goddamn you, I wasn't ready!" His eyes locked with mine. He died with my hand held as firmly as a grouse in his jaws, yet was careful not to hurt me even in his very last moment of life. The spirit of Barney vanished, and he was utterly limp.

In his last split second of life, in that instant when he felt his death, had he felt betrayed? My grief was heightened by a sense of horror over what I had done. I had let the 5:00 closing hour influence my decision. He might have spent one more night at home with me.

I had a little nursery rhyme that I had sung to Barney. It went:

*My Barney lies over the ocean,*
*My Barney lies over the sea.*
*My Barney lies over the ocean,*
*Please bring back my Barney to me.*

...Now, suddenly, he was across an ocean. How I wished I could have him back, if only for one more night. Of the place where Barney's spirit had gone— as with the spirits of all who die among dogs and men—we on this earth know absolutely nothing....

Anyone who has deeply loved a dog knows that, when communication between a person and a dog reaches a certain level, the two regard each other as equals. No one who has ever lived with a Barney would decree that Man alone is of celestial origin, while all other creatures are of earthly origin. Barney was certainly my equal in terms of character and, in terms of being able to give unconditional love, was definitely my better. He put the lie to that arrogant

and outdated dogma asserting that Man alone has a
soul, and that Man alone can reason....

The morning after Barney was put to sleep, I
wrapped him in a blanket and put him into my large
backpack. Joy, Dad, Jimmy Holt, Everette Daught-
ridge, and I drove to Virginia's Smith River, an hour
north of Greensboro. We all walked along the river to
the pool where Barney and I had spent so many hours
fly fishing during the last six winters and springs.

There is an acre of flat ground overlooking a sec-
tion of the river where Barney and I had shared many
a can of cold beans for lunch. As we worked with
pick and shovel to dig Barney's grave, Everette finally
said, "Don't bury him too deep. He won't be able to
hear the river."

At the grave side I quoted the little dog poem that
I had found years ago in Dad's handwriting on the
back cover of the *Georgia-Florida Field Trial Book,* with
the initials "BCB."

> *Oh God, my master,*
> *should I gain the grace*
> *to see thee face to face*
> *when life is ended,*

*grant that a little dog who once pretended*
*that I was God,*
*might see me face to face.*

We dug Barney's grave in February, at the base of two trees that came out of the earth as one. The hickory and the poplar, each a foot and a half through the center, are fused together like lovers. I have never seen two trees, particularly of different species, so joined. Yet their energies are compatible, for they flourish. It seemed an appropriate place to bury my canine partner....

I once had a teacher who bounded through life with great style. He showed me with every hour that the true riches of life, the old verities of pleasure, loyalty, and courage, are literally in front of one's nose. They cannot be bought. Barney's love enabled me to do things I only imagined I was doing alone. As one grows older, one grows wiser.

# Elegy for a Beagle Mutt

LIZ ROSENBERG

1986

HAT A SEASON *this is:*
*darkness making its sure descent, the motley rose*
*of drooping head, and wet leaves plastered*
*everywhere*
*in bright chaotic paths. My leaping pup—*
*she of the quick pulse coiled*
*on the bed who slept in outlandish,*
*graceful twists of the neck,*
*shook by the door, lay dripping on the porch,*
*broke the spines of rabbits and squirrels,*
*begged at every table, that last morning*
*rose from the foot of the bed*
*thrusting her jaw into my face to stare:*
*stern, puzzled, forgiving glance, crushed*
*under a school bus, gone.*
*The sprawl of bones with pomp and grief*
*is laid to rest beneath a rusty tree—*
*and still I see her low shape moving*

*cautiously through every raining bush*
*or flashing under weeds as flaps of newspaper blow by.*
*If I had been out walking,*
*if I had thrown myself into her childish play,*
*she who skittered and obeyed could have led me,*
*licking the hand of every passing soul, and pulled me*
*willy-nilly through the final gate. Now the corpse*
    *commands*
*and I stay here, reminded of the Buddhist saint*
*who waited at the gates of heaven*
*ten thousand years with his faithful dog, till both*
*were permitted in. Lithe dancer, I am reeling on a planet*
*gone to dark moods and imbalance, silent and unsafe,*
*imagining your collar of bones hooked small*
*under my fist—wait for me!*

# The Rainbow Bridge

ANONYMOUS

DATE UNKNOWN

 HERE IS A BRIDGE *connecting heaven and earth.*
*It is called the Rainbow Bridge because of its*
*many colors.*

*Just this side of the Rainbow Bridge there is a land*
*of meadows,*
*hills and valleys with lush green grass.*
*When a beloved pet dies, the pet goes to this special place.*
*There is always food and water and warm spring weather.*
*The old and frail animals are young again.*
*Those who are maimed are made whole again.*
*They play all day with each other.*
*There is only one thing missing.*
*They are not with their special person who loved them*
*on Earth.*
*So each day they run and play until the day comes*
*when one suddenly stops playing and looks up!*
*The nose twitches! The ears are up!*

The eyes are staring! And this one suddenly runs from the
  group!
You have been seen, and when you and your special friend
  meet,
you take him or her into your arms and embrace.
Your face is kissed again and again and again,
and you look once more into the eyes of your trusting pet.
Then you cross the Rainbow Bridge together, never again to
  be separated.

# His Apologies

RUDYARD KIPLING

*ca.* 1934

 ASTER, *this is Thy Servant. He is rising eight
weeks old.
He is mainly Head and Tummy. His legs are
uncontrolled.
But Thou has forgiven his ugliness, and settled him on
Thy knee.
Art Thou content with Thy Servant? He is* **very** *comfy
with Thee.*

*Master, behold a Sinner? He hath done grievous wrong.
He hath defiled Thy Premises through being kept in
too long.
Wherefore his nose has been rubbed in the dirt, and his
self-respect has been bruiséd.
Master, pardon Thy Sinner, and see he is properly looséd.*

*Master—again Thy Sinner! This that was once Thy Shoe,
He hath found and taken and carried aside, as fitting
matter to chew.*

Now there is neither blacking nor tongue, and the
    Housemaid has us in tow.
Master, remember Thy Servant is young, and tell her to let
    him go!

Master, extol Thy Servant! He hath met a most Worthy Foe!
There has been fighting all over the Shop—and into the
    Shop also!
Till cruel umbrellas parted the strife (or I might have been
    choking him yet.)

But Thy Servant has had the Time of his Life—and now
shall we call on the vet?


Master, behold Thy Servant! Strange children came to play,
And because they fought to caress him, Thy Servant
wentedst away.
But now that the Little Beasts have gone, he has returned
to see
(Brushed—with his Sunday collar on—) what they left
over from tea.


Master, pity Thy Servant! He is deaf and three parts blind,
He cannot catch Thy Commandments. He cannot read
Thy Mind.
Oh, leave him not in his loneliness; nor make him that
kitten's scorn.
He has had none other God than Thee since the year that
he was born!


Lord, look down on Thy Servant! Bad things have come
to pass,
There is no heat in the midday sun nor health in the
wayside grass.

*His bones are full of an old disease—his torments run*
*and increase.*
*Lord, make haste with Thy Lightnings and grant him a*
*quick release!*

# Farewell

*from Bob, the Spaniel*

BLANCHE SHOEMAKER WAGSTAFF

1927

 HE DOG IS MAN'S BEST FRIEND. He is the only living creature that thinks more of his master than of himself. He will follow to the grave and remain faithful long afterward. He will risk his life to save. His love will endure to the end. He asks little and gives all. He is the one comrade to be trusted forever.

Dogs do not derive their nobility from association with men. Their intelligence may have advanced beyond that of other animals due to their companionship with human beings. But their qualities of loyalty, unselfishness, service, resignation and compassion are peculiar to their kind.

Dog's lives are rarely happy. At the whim of a master who may, at any moment, send them away to another part of the world,—how uncertain and anxious must be their existence! When we leave them, what assurance have they of our return? How little certitude or peace must be theirs in their brief span of years amongst us! A short space and a nameless grave awaiting them,—so much beloved, so soon forgotten.

Unwavering friends of man, what is their reward? How kind we should be to these dumb creatures. Sent amongst us unbidden,—what gentleness and understanding we should give them,—their loyalty and patience and love, gifts we cannot value too highly in this world of ephemeral things. How sweet is the flower of their fellowship,—how rare their everlasting devotion!

None will love us as the dog. None will give to us the boundless, blind affection, forgiving us our foibles and follies. Even in slumber we are unforgotten; our footstep sends them trembling with happiness; our departure leaves them disconsolate. Around us their life revolves, wanting no other happiness but our presence.

O most compassionate and tenderest of creatures, O understanding heart of a little dog, divining our slightest wish, sharing our secret sorrow, wanting only to serve us with silent submission,—unknown to guile or malice,——what tributes have we that are worthy of you? What can we give you commensurate with your gifts to us?

In another world may the little dog heart know happiness and rest. Many believe that dogs inhabit heaven. I hope it is so. And in that last golden hour, when we all stand together, may we look again upon the faces of our pets, our lost devoted ones; little dog souls returned again to welcome us from the great dark Silence...and how glad we shall be to greet their patient faces in that land where dreams come true, in that realm of peace and rest where we may be once more beside our loyal comrade and friend, the dog.

# The House Dog's Grave

ROBINSON JEFFERS

1941

'VE CHANGED *my ways a little; I cannot now*
*Run with you in the evenings along the shore,*
*Except in a kind of dream; and you, if you*
    *dream a moment,*
*You see me there.*

*So leave awhile the paw-marks on the front door*
*Where I used to scratch to go out or in,*
*And you'd soon open; leave on the kitchen floor*
*The marks of my drinking-pan.*

*I cannot lie by your fire as I used to do*
*On the warm stone,*
*Nor at the foot of your bed; no, all the night through*
*I lie alone.*

*But your kind thought has laid me less than six feet*
*Outside your window where firelight so often plays,*

And where you sit to read—and I fear often grieving
   for me—
Every night your lamplight lies on my place.

You, man and woman, live so long, it is hard
To think of you ever dying
A little dog would get tired, living so long.
I hope that when you are lying

Under the ground like me your lives will appear
As good and joyful as mine.
No, dear, that's too much hope: you are not so well cared for
As I have been.

And never have known the passionate undivided
Fidelities that I knew.
Your minds are perhaps too active, too many-sided....
But to me you were true.

You were never masters, but friends. I was your friend.
I loved you well, and was loved. Deep love endures
To the end and far past the end. If this is my end,
I am not lonely. I am not afraid. I am still yours.

# Epitaph for a Small Dog

LE BARON COOKE

*ca.* 1935

**H**ERE RESTS *a little dog*
*Whose feet ran never faster*
Than when they took the path
Leading to his master.

The Dog's Cemetery, Hyde Park, London.

# The Vicar's Tribute:
# "Plum-Pudding's Epitaph"

GEORGE ARBUTHNOT,
VICAR OF TRINITY CHURCH
STRATFORD-ON-AVON
*ca.* 1920

 "PUDDING!" *companion of my parish round,*
*Content to walk to heel or patient wait,*
*Eager to follow, and yet always found*
*Watching attentive at the sick man's gate:*
*Thy task is done, and through the busy mart,*
*The idler sees thee thread thy way no more,*
*But I, who know thy faithful, loving heart,*
*Expect to meet thee at the Heavenly door.*

# Request from the Rainbow Bridge

CONSTANCE JENKINS
*in loving memory of Isolde Jenkins*
1995

 EEP NOT *for me though I am gone*
*Into that gentle night.*
*Grieve if you will, but not for long*
*Upon my soul's sweet flight.*
*I am at peace, my soul's at rest,*
*There is no need for tears.*
*For with your love I was so blessed*
*for all those many years.*
*There is no pain, I suffer not,*
*The fear now all is gone.*
*Put now these things out of your*
*   thoughts.*
*In your memory I live on.*
*Remember not my fight for breath,*
*Remember not the strife.*
*Please do not dwell upon my death,*
*But celebrate my life.*

# Finale

BURGESS JOHNSON
1935

LEEK SABLE *Ozra, royal Dane,*
  *Small Jetsam, of strange pedigree,*
  *Bolo, who crossed the Spanish main,*
*And shy, devoted, Scotch Dundee,*

*And all that eager, trusting band*
  *Who lived their lives as best they knew;*
*Who thrust wet muzzles 'gainst my hand,*
  *And gave me love beyond my due;*

*So gallantly each played his part*
  *That no new friend usurps his place.*
*In quiet corners of my heart*
  *Each owns, still warm, a bedding-space.*

*I'll not believe their jaunty tails*
  *Are drooping in Death's gloomy pound,—*
*But one by one they found the trails*
  *That lead to some far hunting ground.*

*I hope it breaks no holy laws*
  *If 'neath God's table they are fed;*
*I like to think their spirit paws*
  *May dig Elysium's garden bed.*

*And He who fashioned grass and trees,*
  *And cares for sparrows, beasts and men,*
*May let them press against His knees*
  *And stoop to stroke them now and then.*

# PET LOSS RESOURCES

## Pet Loss Support Groups

A *Directory of Pet Loss Resources*, including a list of pet loss counselors, telephone hotlines, and support groups throughout the U.S. is available from the Delta Society, 289 Perimeter Road East, Renton, WA 98055-1329, for $3.00. The Delta Society also has several videotapes on pet loss and bereavement available for rental or purchase.

## Pet Loss Support Hotline

University of California, Davis, Pet Loss Support Hotline, (916) 752-4200, 6:30-9:30 PM Monday through Friday, Pacific time. Pet loss support hotlines are also available at other major veterinary schools throughout the United States.

## Published Pet Memorials

Rainbow Bridge Memorials are published monthly in *Best Friends* magazine, with a donation to Best Friends Animal Sanctuary, the largest no-kill animal sanctuary in the U.S. Photographs may be included. Send to Best Friends Animal Sanctuary, Kanab, UT 84741. (801) 644-2001.

## Pet Cemeteries

For information about pet cemeteries, contact The Accredited Pet Cemeteries Society, 139 West Rush Rd., West Rush, NY 14543;

(716) 533-1685, or International Association of Pet Cemeteries, Route 11, Box 163, Ellensburg Depot, NY 12935; (518) 594-3000.

## On the Internet

Rainbow Bridge Tribute Pages:

http://www.primenet.com/~Meggie/bridge.htm

Pet Loss Grief Support Page and Candle Ceremony:

http://www.petloss.com

Virtual Pet Cemetery:

http://www.pet@lavamind.com

## Recommended Books on Pet Loss

Herb & Mary Montgomery. *Goodbye My Friend: Grieving the Loss of a Pet.* Minneapolis: Montgomery Press, 1991.

*A Final Act of Caring: Ending the Life of an Animal Friend.* Minneapolis: Montgomery Press, 1993.

Linda M. Peterson. *Surviving the Heartbreak of Choosing Death for Your Pet: Your Personal Guide for Dealing with Pet Euthanasia.* West Chester, PA: Greentree Publishing, 1997.

Cynthia Rylant. *Dog Heaven.* New York: Scholastic Books, 1996. (childrens' book)

## Recommended Reading on the Human-Animal Bond

Marjorie Garber, *Dog Love.* New York: Simon & Schuster, 1996.

Jeffrey Mousaieff Masson, *Dogs Never Lie About Love: Reflections on the Emotional World of Dogs.* New York: Crown Publishers, 1997.

Susan Chernak McElroy, *Animals as Teachers and Healers: True Stories and Reflections.* New York: Ballantine Books, 1997.

Mary Elizabeth Thurston, *The Lost History of the Canine Race: Our 15,000 Year Love Affair with Dogs.* Kansas City: Andrews and McMeel, 1996.

# ACKNOWLEDGMENTS
# & BIBLIOGRAPHY

THE EDITOR gratefully acknowledges the assistance of the following persons whose contributions made this book possible. For
guidance and encouragement, editorial review, and insightful
comments on the draft manuscript, I am indebted to Victoria
Coulter, Elaine Sichel, Jim Simmerman, and Randy Varney. Teddi
Thomas, Jane Handel, Sandy Milns, and Sherry Sonnett helped
locate many wonderful vintage photographs of dogs. As the
book's designer, Troy Scott Parker solved the challenges of work-
ing with antique photographs, and was a creative partner on the
project. My husband, John Peel, provided encouragement, fixed
dinner, and ignored the heaps of work in progress. And finally,
my three springer spaniels, Chester, Dixie, and Byron, who were
at my feet as I worked, to whom I am grateful every day for their
love and companionship.

&#x6d;&#x6d;

The Editor has made every effort to locate the owners of copyrighted material and to secure permission to reprint. Permission
to reprint copyrighted material is gratefully acknowledged
below. All other material is believed to be in the public domain.

George Arbuthnot. "The Vicar's Tribute." In *Songs of Dogs, an Anthology Selected and Arranged by Robert Frothingham*. Boston: Houghton Mifflin, 1920.

Katherine Lee Bates. "To Sigourd." Frothingham, *Songs of Dogs*.

Ethel Blumann. "So Long, Pal." In *Your Dog and My Dog: from Tony Wons Famous Radio Scrapbook,* compiled by Anthony Wons. Chicago: Reilly & Lee, 1935.

C. Hilton Brown. "Hamish—A Scotch Terrier." Frothingham, *Songs of Dogs*. Originally appeared in *London Spectator,* n.d.

Fred H. Clifford. "Only a Dog." Wons, *Your Dog and My Dog*.

Le Baron Cooke. "Epitaph for a Small Dog." Wons, *Your Dog and My Dog*.

Ruth Pollak Coughlin. "Lucy Never Had a Bone to Pick—She Loved Unconditionally." *Detroit News,* 1992. Used by permission.

Reverend Julian S. Cutler. "Roger and I." Frothingham, *Songs of Dogs*. Originally published in the *Boston Evening Transcript,* n.d.

Paul de Lott. "Just a Dog!" Wons, *Your Dog and My Dog*.

Grace Strong Dignowity. "To Roxy." Wons, *Your Dog and My Dog*.

Walter A. Dyer. "The Prayer of a Pup." Wons, *Your Dog and My Dog*. Originally published in *Gulliver the Great and Other Dog Stories,* n.d.

John Galsworthy. *Memories*. New York: Charles Scribner's Sons, 1914.

Lars Gustaffson. "Elegy for a Dead Labrador." Translated by Yvonne L. Sandstroem. From *The Stillness of the World Before Bach*. Copyright © 1980 by Lars Gustaffson and Yvonne L. Sandstroem. Reprinted by permission of New Directions Publishing Corporation.

James Clarence Harvey. "Laddie's Long Sleep." Frothingham, *Songs of Dogs*.

Norah M. Holland. "Little Dog Angel." Wons, *Your Dog and My Dog*.

Robinson Jeffers. "The House Dog's Grave." In *Be Angry at the Sun*. New York: Random House, 1941.

Constance Jenkins. "Request From the Rainbow Bridge." *Best Friends,* February 1995. Kanab, Utah: Best Friends Animal Sanctuary. Copyright © 1995 by Constance Jenkins. Used by permission.

Burgess Johnson. "Finale." In *Sonnets from the Pekinese and Other Doggerel.* New York: Macmillan, 1935.

Lincoln Kinnicutt. "Dear Dogs." In *To Your Dog and To My Dog,* ed. Lincoln Kinnicutt. Boston: Houghton Mifflin, 1915.

Rudyard Kipling. "Dinah in Heaven." In *Collected Dog Stories by Rudyard Kipling.* London: World Books, 1934.

Rudyard Kipling. "The Power of the Dog." Kipling, *Collected Dog Stories.*

Rudyard Kipling. "His Apologies." Kipling, *Collected Dog Stories.*

Alphonse de Lamartine. "O Dog of Mine." In *Faithful to the End,* by Celia Haddon. New York: St. Martins Press, 1991. Used by permission.

Ben Hur Lampman. "Where to Bury a Dog." Originally appeared in *The Oregonian,* copyright 1925, 1953 by Oregonian Publishing. Used by permission.

Robert C. Lehmann. "A Retriever's Epitaph." In *Dogs Book of Verse,* collected by J. Earl Clauson. Boston: Small Maynard & Co., 1916.

St. John Lucas. "My Dog." Kinnicutt, *To Your Dog and To My Dog.*

Susan Chernak McElroy. "Going Gently: Love, Loss, and Death." In *Animals as Teachers and Healers,* by Susan McElroy. New York: Ballantine Press, 1997. Copyright © 1996, 1997 by Susan Chernak McElroy. Used by permission of Ballantine Books, a division of Random House, Inc.

"An Old Dog." Anonymous. Kinnicutt, *To Your Dog and To My Dog.*

Eugene O'Neill. "The Last Will & Testament of Silverdene Emblem O'Neill." In *The Unknown O'Neill,* ed. Travis Bogard. Copyright © 1988 Yale University Press. Used by permission.

"The Passing of a Dog." Anonymous. Clauson, *Dog's Book of Verse.*

Walter Peirce. "To John, My Collie." Frothingham, *Songs of Dogs.* Originally appeared in *Country Gentleman,* n.d.

H.I. Phillips. "The Death of a Dog." In *A Treasury of the Dog,* ed. Ralph Woods, New York: G.P. Putnam, 1956. Originally published in the *New York World-Telegram,* November 8, 1955.

"The Rainbow Bridge." Author and source unknown.

Liz Rosenberg. "Elegy for a Beagle Mutt." In *Dog Music: Poetry About Dogs,* ed. Joseph Duemer and Jim Simmerman. New York: St. Martins Press, 1996. Originally published in *The Fire Music,* by Liz Rosenberg. Copyright ©1986. Used by permission of the University of Pittsburgh Press.

John D. Rucker. *The Barney Years.* Minocqua, WI: NorthWord Press, 1992. Copyright © 1992 John D. Rucker. Used by permission.

Jim Simmerman. "Fetch." In Duemer and Simmerman, *Dog Music.* Originally published in *Once Out of Nature,* copyright © 1989 by Jim Simmerman. Used by permission of Galileo Press and the author.

Jim Simmerman. "Maddy's Woods." In Duemer and Simmerman, *Dog Music.* First published in *Moon Go Away, I Don't Love You No More,* copyright © 1994, Miami University Press. Used by permission.

Kate Clark Spencer. "When I Died on My Birthday." In *Unleashed: Poems by Writers' Dogs,* ed. Amy Hempel and Jim Shepard. New York: Crown Publishers, 1995. Copyright © 1995 by Amy Hempel and Jim Shepard. Used by permission.

James Thurber. "Memorial." In *Thurber's Dogs.* New York: Simon & Schuster, 1942. Copyright © 1942 by James Thurber. Copyright © 1970 by Helen Thurber and Rosemary A. Thurber. Reprinted by arrangement with Rosemary A. Thurber and the Barbara Hogenson Agency.

"To a Dog." Anonymous. Clauson, *Dog's Book of Verse.*

H.P.W. "Jack." Clauson, *Dog's Book of Verse.*

Blanche Shoemaker Wagstaff. "Farewell." In *Bob, the Spaniel: the True Story of a Springer.* New York: G. Howard Watt, 1927.

Richard Wightman. "Frances." Frothingham, *Songs of Dogs.* Originally published in *Ashes and Sparks,* Century Company, n.d.

Henry Willett. "In Memoriam." Clauson, *Dog's Book of Verse.*

William Hervey Woods. "In the Mansion Yard." Frothingham, *Songs of Dogs.* Originally appeared in *Scribner's Magazine,* n.d.

**DARROWBY PRESS**
3510 Thorndale Road
Pasadena, California 91107, USA
Phone & Fax 626-792-7387

Please send _____ copies of *Angel Pawprints* at $15.95 each.
Add $4.50 Priority Mail postage and handling for the first book and
75¢ for each additional book.

*For books shipped to California addresses, please add California state sales tax.*

Name: _____

Address: _____

City, State, ZIP: _____

Please charge my:

☐ Visa   ☐ MasterCard   #: _____

Expiration date: _____

Signature: _____

Enclosed is my check or money order for: $_____

☐ This is a gift. Please send directly to:

Name: _____

Address: _____

City, State, ZIP: _____

Inscription (use additional space if needed): _____

_____

☐ Please send information on additional pet loss resources available from
Darrowby Press.